ECONOMICS OF ENTERTAINMENT
THE ECONOMICS OF A VIDEO GAME

Kathryn Hulick

Crabtree Publishing Company
www.crabtreebooks.com

Author: Kathryn Hulick
Editor-in-chief: Lionel Bender
Editors: Simon Adams, Rachel Eagen
Proofreaders: Laura Booth, Wendy Scavuzzo
Project coordinator: Kathy Middleton
Design and photo research: Ben White
Cover design: Margaret Amy Salter
Production: Kim Richardson
Print and production coordinator:
   Margaret Amy Salter
Prepress technician: Margaret Amy Salter

Consultant: Laura Ebert, Ph.D., Lecturer in
Economics at the State University of New
York at New Paltz, N.Y.
Industry consultant: Jen MacLean, former
CEO, 38 Studios

This book was produced for
Crabtree Publishing Company
by Bender Richardson White.

Photographs and reproductions:
Getty Images: 6 bottom right (Getty Images), 8–9 (AFP/Getty
Images), 12–13 (Getty Images), 20–21 (Future/Getty Images), 24–25
(Bloomberg via Getty Images), 26–27 (Getty Images), 28–29 (Alberto
E. Rodriguez), 30–31 (Blend Images/John Fedele), 32–33 AFP/Getty
Images), 34–35 (Bloomberg via Getty Images), 38–39 (Getty
Images). Shutterstock.com: cover-center and top inset (Barone
Firenze), banners (NesaCera), icons (igorlale, greglith, DM7,
Lusoimages, Christopher Meder, Julien_N, koya979, Nomad_Soul),
1 (CREATISTA) , 4–5 (Barone Firenze), 6–7 (1000 Words), 10–11
(DarkGeometryStudios), 13 (zeber), 14–15 (iurii), 16–17 bottom
middle (Barone Firenze), 17 top left (Andresr), 18–19 (Jorg
Hackemann), 22–23 (Barone Firenze), 26 (Maxim Blinkov), 34
(fkdkondmi), 36–37 (NesaCera), 40–41 (Przemek Tokar), 42 top left
(Nomad_Soul), 42–43 (Victor Habbick), 43 top right (bloom).
Wikimedia Commons: cover-bottom inset (David Becker), cover-left
inset (Pam Mayer (pamnesiac))
Sony, PlayStation, Nintendo, Apple, iPhone, iPad, Atari, Xbox, Wii,
Microsoft, Activision and other games manufacturers and brands
are registered trademarks and/or protected by copyright and
usually given with ™, ®, or © symbol.

Graphics: Stefan Chabluk

Library and Archives Canada Cataloguing in Publication

Hulick, Kathryn, author
    The economics of a video game / Kathryn Hulick.

(Economics of entertainment)
Includes index.
Issued in print and electronic formats.
ISBN 978-0-7787-7970-4 (bound).--ISBN 978-0-7787-7975-9 (pbk.).--
ISBN 978-1-4271-7869-5 (pdf).--ISBN 978-1-4271-7984-5 (html)

    1. Video games--Economic aspects--Juvenile literature.
2. Video games industry--Juvenile literature. I. Title.

GV1469.34.E3H85 2014   j794.8   C2013-907579-8
                                               C2013-907580-1

Library of Congress Cataloging-in-Publication Data

Hulick, Kathryn.
 The economics of a video game / Kathryn Hulick.
    pages cm. -- (Economics of entertainment)
 Includes index.
 ISBN 978-0-7787-7970-4 (reinforced library binding) -- ISBN
978-0-7787-7975-9 (pbk.) -- ISBN 978-1-4271-7869-5 (electronic
pdf) -- ISBN 978-1-4271-7984-5 (electronic html)
1. Video games--Economic aspects--Juvenile literature. 2.
Video games industry--Juvenile literature. I. Title.

 HD9993.E452H85 2014
 338.4'77948--dc23
                                               2013043402

Crabtree Publishing Company

www.crabtreebooks.com   1-800-387-7650

Printed in Canada/022014/MA20131220

Published in Canada
Crabtree Publishing
616 Welland Ave.
St. Catharines, ON
L2M 5V6

Published in the United States
Crabtree Publishing
PMB 59051
350 Fifth Avenue, 59th Floor
New York, New York 10118

Published in the United Kingdom
Crabtree Publishing
Maritime House
Basin Road North, Hove
BN41 1WR

Published in Australia
Crabtree Publishing
3 Charles Street
Coburg North
VIC, 3058

CONTENTS

VIDEONOMICS

Quick! Jump over the pit of lava and dodge that bad guy. Video games are fun to play, but did you ever wonder how a brand new game got into your hands? Sure, you bought it at the store but, at some point, it was just an idea in someone's head. **Economics** helps explain the choices that are made along the journey from idea to finished game.

This PlayStation Vita strategy game forces the player to make choices about how to use scarce resources.

BASIC ECONOMICS

Canada, the United States, England, Japan, Germany, and many other countries follow an economic system called **capitalism**. In this system, governments do not control most businesses and resources. Instead, people buy and sell as they wish in a free market.

A BRAND NEW GAME

Economics is a system that helps **resources** (for example, water), **services** (such as education), and **goods** (such as video games) get from **producers** to **consumers** (the people who use them—like you!). When you buy or download a game, you're taking part in the economy. Consumers decide freely how to spend their money, and the companies choose how much the products should cost. In this type of system, called a **market economy**, everyone involved has the freedom to make his or her decision.

DIFFICULT DECISIONS

The tricky part is that there isn't always enough of the resources, services, and goods that we want and need. This is called **scarcity**. When you want to buy a new game but don't have enough money, then money is scarce for you. Often, when you're playing a video game, your character doesn't have enough health or spell power—this is scarcity, too. Scarcity forces you to make difficult choices. Often, these hard choices are what make a video game so much fun! Playing games can teach you about economics.

WHAT DO YOU THINK?

You can learn about economics when playing a game. What resources are scarce in your favorite game? How does scarcity make the game better?

FOOTBALL OR DRAGONS?

How do you decide whether to buy a $60 football game or download a cheap fantasy game and also buy a cool T-shirt? In this decision, you have to make a tradeoff: If you spend the money on the football game, then you can't spend that same money on anything else. The fun you will have playing the fantasy game and wearing the T-shirt, in this example, is the **opportunity cost** of buying the football game. An opportunity cost is what you have lost by making a different choice.

Of course, price can also influence your decision. If the football game costs $30, you might buy an extra copy for a friend! Consumers all have a certain amount of disposable income, or money left over after paying taxes. This amount helps determine what prices a consumer can afford.

If the price of a good falls, and income and choices remain the same, people will buy more of that good. This is the law of **demand**. But how much will demand rise? A little or a lot? The price **elasticity** of demand is a measure of how a change in price affects your behavior. Generally, luxury goods such as video games and movies have elastic prices, meaning that small price shifts lead to large changes in demand.

CASTING YOUR VOTE

Your choice makes a difference in the economy. **Consumer sovereignty** is the idea that people like you control what companies make. How does that work? If every child decided to buy football games instead of fantasy games, companies wouldn't make any money trying to sell fantasy games. Goodbye, dragons! In a way, when you choose to buy a game, you are casting a vote for that particular product.

WHAT DO YOU THINK?

Would an iPhone game or a gallon of milk have a more elastic price, and why? Which one do you want and which do you need?

The choice you make to buy a certain video game matters in the economy.

HOW MUCH MONEY DO WE SPEND ON GAMES?

+10%
spending on
Microsoft
Xbox 360
games

+8%
spending
on
digital
content

2010
$32

2011
$32

-10%
spending
on
Wii games

-8%
spending on
new and used
boxed games
and rentals

In both 2010 and 2011, people who bought games spent an average of U.S. $32 per month on them. But the way they spent that $32 changed.

Shoppers enter an Apple store. The iPhone and iPad are two of the top bestselling products of all time.

① VIDEO GAME INDUSTRY

People love playing games! In 2012, people in the United States spent a total of $20.77 billion on video games, including game systems, accessories, and the games themselves. Games that come in a box still make the most money, but free and cheap downloadable games are changing the game industry.

SHIGI
MIYA
Senior Managing D
Nintendo Co., Ltd.

Video game designer Shigeru Miyamoto, creator of the *Mario* games, takes the stage in Los Angeles.

THE FIRST VIDEO GAMES

Have you heard of *Pong*? Electronics manufacturer Atari released this video game in 1972. Players had to bat a ball back and forth on a boxy screen with just two colors. It was a simple game, but people loved it! In 1985, the Nintendo Entertainment System (NES) brought video games such as *Mario* and *Zelda* into people's homes. Early games didn't have lifelike graphics or movie-style special effects, but they still presented challenging obstacles and tested players' skills.

GAMES, GAMES EVERYWHERE!

Video games today are much more than just something you play alone while sitting at home. Games and gaming systems are now portable, so you can carry them around in your backpack and play them on mobile phones, tablets, laptop computers, and handheld gaming devices. Some games involve dancing, singing, or swinging a controller. Other games connect you to a network of friends, allowing you to play together even if you live many miles apart.

A RISKY BUSINESS

Making games is a risky business. It costs millions of dollars to produce a full Xbox or PlayStation game. The game publisher has to sell hundreds of thousands of games to make a **profit**. Profit is how much money the company has left over when you subtract the money the company spent to make the game (the **cost**) from the money people paid for the game (the **revenue**). The game is a success for the company only if revenues are higher than costs.

SUPPLY AND DEMAND

Video game companies want to make as much revenue as possible. So why don't they charge more for games? One reason is that people who are interested in games might not be able to afford the higher price. Other types of entertainment, such as movies or books, will seem like a better deal. The law of demand states that as prices rise, the number of goods people will buy drops.

Remember that games tend to have elastic prices, meaning that demand is very sensitive to changes in price. Doctor's visits, on the other hand, tend to have inelastic prices, meaning that the price can change without affecting demand very much. If you need a cast for a broken leg, your family will find a way to pay the price.

Elastic prices mean that charging less for something can actually earn the company more money because so many more people will buy it. Elasticity is one possible reason that many downloadable games for smartphones and tablets cost $0.99. Cheaper games mean a huge increase in the number of downloads.

U.S. COMPUTER AND VIDEO GAME SALES

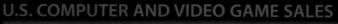

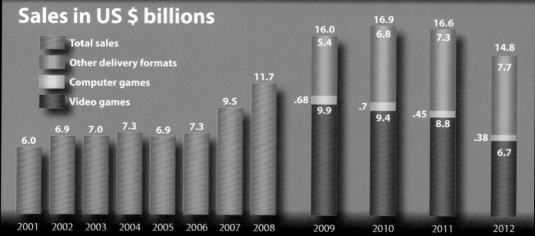

Sales in US $ billions

- Total sales
- Other delivery formats
- Computer games
- Video games

Year	Total sales	Other delivery formats	Computer games	Video games
2001	6.0			
2002	6.9			
2003	7.0			
2004	7.3			
2005	6.9			
2006	7.3			
2007	9.5			
2008	11.7			
2009	16.0	5.4	.68	9.9
2010	16.9	6.8	.7	9.4
2011	16.6	7.3	.45	8.8
2012	14.8	7.7	.38	6.7

Total sales of games have increased massively in recent years.

The graphics and animation of video games are as sophisticated as science-fiction movies.

FINDING EQUILIBRIUM

Why aren't all games super-cheap? It's because of **supply**, which is the opposite of demand. Supply is the number of games that companies make to sell at a certain price. If prices fall, companies can't make as much money from each sale, so they make fewer games. Fewer games at lower prices means demand starts to rise, then companies can charge more again.

Over time, markets tend to find a price where supply and demand are roughly equal. At this equilibrium, or balance point, enough people who want the game can buy it and the game companies are making enough money to stay in business.

THE RECORD BREAKERS

Players pay a fee each month to build characters and complete quests in *World of Warcraft*. The game has made over $10 billion in revenue.

GAME PLATFORMS

ALL THE EXTRAS

Anyone can buy a book and start reading it right away but, to play a video game, you need to own a device first. How many smartphones, computers, and video-game consoles does your family have? The average household has at least one of these devices and more than 50 percent own a console that is used only for games.

The markets for mobile games, computer games, and console games are all different. Console games still make more money than any other part of the game market. These games could not exist without the console industry. People won't buy a brand new console unless they can buy really great games to go with it. Game companies will only make games for a console if they think enough people will buy the device.

WHAT DO YOU THINK?

If your family can afford only one console and you get a new PlayStation 4, then you can't play games made for the Xbox One. What is the opportunity cost of buying PlayStation 4?

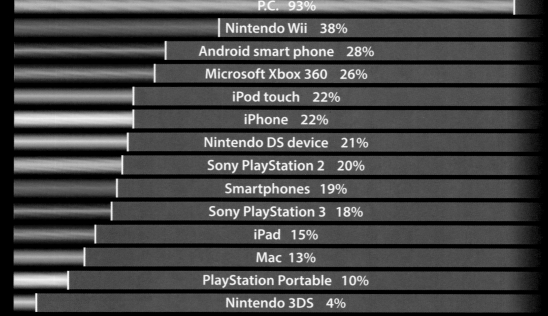

GAME PLATFORMS IN U.S. HOMES (as percentage of all homes, 2012)

- P.C. 93%
- Nintendo Wii 38%
- Android smart phone 28%
- Microsoft Xbox 360 26%
- iPod touch 22%
- iPhone 22%
- Nintendo DS device 21%
- Sony PlayStation 2 20%
- Smartphones 19%
- Sony PlayStation 3 18%
- iPad 15%
- Mac 13%
- PlayStation Portable 10%
- Nintendo 3DS 4%

More than half of all U.S. households own a video-game console. Which platforms do you have at home?

THE BIG THREE

Sony makes the PlayStation and Vita, Microsoft makes the Xbox, and Nintendo makes the Wii and DS series. These three companies form an **oligopoly** because they control almost the entire game-console market. In an oligopoly, if each company keeps prices high, then the whole group benefits. But if one company lowers prices, a price war may follow. Console prices are very competitive, and a company may even lose money each time it sells a console. But the company will make that money back from sales of video games made for their console.

Adults aged 25–34 play more smartphone games than any other age group.

The average person plays games for seven hours a week.

FROM IDEA TO DEVELOPMENT

Every game you play began as an idea. But most ideas never make it into production, or "off the drawing board." Building a game takes time, money, and a lot of work. The first step in making a video game is to predict whether it will be a success. The company will predict how many games it might sell based on how many copies of similar games it sold in the past. If it thinks it can make more money in revenues than it will spend in costs, then it's game on!

INSIDER INSIGHT

"We have to be passionate about what we create. What excites us? What keeps us up at night? We also look at the market—do we think it will make money?"
Ichiro Lambe, independent game developer

Most video games are fantasy, sport, or challenge games.

NINJA GECKOS

Let's say that a new Xbox game just came out about *Zuni and the Ninja Geckos*—a band of heroes who battle evil cactus invaders. This game probably didn't start when one person imagined a ninja gecko. More likely, a company knew it wanted to make an action game for Xbox, and this idea won out over many others.

The game characters and their world are **intellectual property**. This is a term for the ideas that belong only to the person or company who created them. In other words, other companies couldn't make products using Zuni the Gecko unless they get permission and pay a **licensing fee**.

THE POWER OF BRANDING

In the game industry, as well as in the book and movie industries, a popular character or world is called a **brand**. Here are some brands you probably recognize: *Super Mario*, *Star Wars*, and *Angry Birds*. Brands have power in a market economy because many people stay loyal to a brand even if other options are cheaper or of a higher quality. You might buy a *Star Wars* game instead of the ninja gecko game because you already love *Star Wars* and you don't know anything about the geckos.

It can be a big gamble to make a game that doesn't have a character or a world that is already a well-known brand. For this reason, series games are common. When a company makes a new series game, it knows that people who loved other games in the series will most likely buy the new game, too.

WHAT DO YOU THINK?

Do you prefer a brand such as PlayStation or Xbox over other similar choices? Why is it important for a company to create brand loyalty?

REVENUES AND COSTS

MAKING A DEAL

Xbox or PlayStation games can cost as much as $100 million or more to make. To help pay the high cost of development, game companies need **funding**, or sources of money, to support building the game.

Game companies, or publishers, such as Nintendo or Sony, usually provide funding to creative people known as game developers. In return, the publisher gets a percentage of the revenues. Sometimes, developers pitch ideas to publishers and, at other times, publishers hire developers to build games for them. The two companies sign a legal contract, or a detailed agreement, that explains how all the costs and revenues will be shared between them.

The publisher often pays the lion's, or bigger, share of the cost of making the game, while the developer does almost all of the work. Since the publisher pays the most money, it also takes on the most financial risk. This means that the publisher will take a bigger loss if the game fails, but it could also make much more profit if the game succeeds.

HIGH RISK, HIGH REWARD

In 2010, the game developer Bungie and the publisher Activision planned to spend three years and $140 million on the first console game in a new series. The game may bring extremely high profits. But if it makes less than $140 million in revenue, the companies will take a **loss**. Despite the risk of taking a loss, many companies see the opportunity for a high financial reward as an **incentive**, or motivation, to make new games.

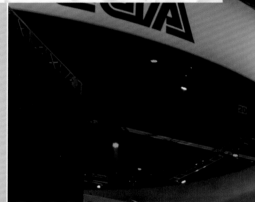

TRICKS OF THE TRADE

In the mobile-game industry, everything is faster and cheaper. A game may take just nine months and $250,000 to develop, but profits (or losses) will usually be lower as well.

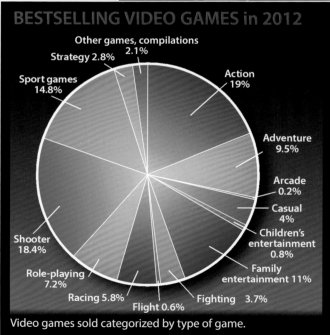

BESTSELLING VIDEO GAMES in 2012

- Other games, compilations 2.1%
- Strategy 2.8%
- Sport games 14.8%
- Action 19%
- Adventure 9.5%
- Arcade 0.2%
- Casual 4%
- Children's entertainment 0.8%
- Family entertainment 11%
- Fighting 3.7%
- Flight 0.6%
- Racing 5.8%
- Role-playing 7.2%
- Shooter 18.4%

Video games sold categorized by type of game.

ABOVE Game publishers must get their finances right.

BELOW *Sonic the Hedgehog*, shown here, is a recognizable brand from Sega.

A CONTRACT FOR "DESTINY" GAME

Publisher Activision and development studio Bungie signed a contract in 2010 for a series of four action games code-named "Destiny." The first game was due out in 2013. Here are some of the key terms in the contract. Figures are in U.S. dollars.

Four games and four expansions in 10 years – Bungie will develop a "Destiny" game every two years starting in 2013. On the off years, Bungie will release an expansion to the game, code named "Comet."

$140 million – the total maximum budget for the first "Destiny" game on Xbox 360, including marketing costs

Activision's profits in one year (revenues minus operating expenses)	Royalties owed to Bungie
$0-$100 million	20%
Over $100 million to $400 million	24%
Over $400 million	35%

$7.5 million – total bonuses Activision will pay Bungie for staying on schedule and on budget during development

$2.5 million – quality bonus Activision will pay Bungie if the game achieves a rating of at least 90 on gamerankings.com

$25 million – bonus Bungie receives if the game makes more than $750 million in profit

$25 million – an additional bonus Bungie receives if Activision makes $1 billion or more in total profits

Fun facts
– Bungie employees will each be entitled to two free Activision games every year
– Bungie has to provide Activision with a list of "Easter Eggs," or game secrets

INSIDER INSIGHT

"In a pitch presentation, you talk about why the game is a great idea, then about the competition, and then about the potential sales."
Jen MacLean, game developer

PREDICTION OR GUESSWORK?

Company executives need to predict how much money a new game might make. But no magic crystal ball can see the future (except maybe in a video game world)! Companies look at the size of their audience and past sales figures for similar games to help make these predictions. If a game costs $60 and will likely sell one million copies, the company can expect $60 million in revenues.

The largest possible audience for the ninja geckos game includes everyone who owns an Xbox and plays action games. But each of the potential customers for the game has a lot of choices and a limited amount of money. The game company needs to convince as many potential buyers that the ninja geckos game is the best choice. If it can do this, demand for the game will increase and sales will go up.

TRICKS OF THE TRADE

Series games are very common because buyers tend to come back for each new game. The publisher EA releases a new *Madden NFL* title each year at the beginning of the new football season. Sales are almost exactly the same from year to year.

AN ECONOMIC BATTLE

Competition is the economic battle between companies trying to sell the same types of products. In a market with perfect competition, companies must lower production costs because their products are the same. If just one company makes a product, this is called a **monopoly**, and competition won't exist.

Many video game companies can't compete on price because the console makers and large video game publishers set the prices. All new games for the same system cost the same amount. All Xbox One, Wii U, and PlayStation 4 games cost about $60. Console games compete with advertising and branding instead of price.

In a sense, a video game company has a monopoly on each game it sells because no one else is making the exact same game. Companies that sell unique but similar products participate in **monopolistic competition**. The ninja gecko game may compete with dozens of other games about heroes that run around fighting bad guys. To win new customers, a game company has to make its story, art, advertising, and packaging stand out from all the other competing games.

Many different companies compete for attention at a shopping complex in Bangkok, Thailand.

WHAT DO YOU THINK?

Can you name three industries where monopolistic competition takes place? Think about "cool" products with brand names that matter more than price.

MADDEN NFL TOTAL GLOBAL SALES

million sales

2008–09	2009–10	2010–11	2011–12	2012–13
2.49	2.79	2.64	2.62	2.46

Madden NFL games are always launched at the end of August or beginning of September, the start of the National Football League season. Sales remain largely consistent year after year.

3 BUILDING A WORLD

In economics, **capital** is anything that helps produce other things. The **physical capital** in video game development includes computers, desks, and software programs. The people who build a game are **human capital**. A video game company needs a team of hard-working people with the right skills and knowledge. That team works together to create a complete and exciting game world within a limited amount of time.

TRICKS OF THE TRADE

Instead of earning salaries, the handful of employees at the independent game studio Dejobaan Games work on **revenue share**. They earn a percentage of the profits for each game they produce.

GAME DEVELOPER SALARIES

Average salary in game industry $84,337	
Executives $103,934	
Programmers $92,151	
Producers $84,127	
Audio professionals $81,543	
Game designers $75,065	
Artists and animators $75,009	
QA testers $48,611	Figures in U.S. dollars. Salaries as in 2012.

Game developers earn good money.

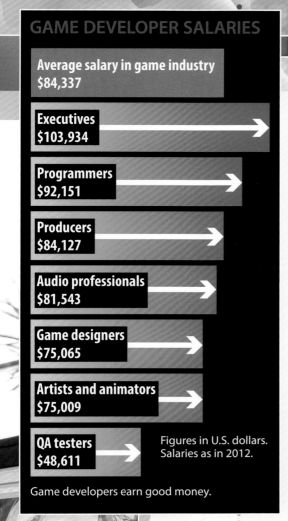

Artist Timm Schwank of German video game design studio Deck 13 works on a game.

CODE, ART, AND FUN

Programmers, artists, and designers make up the core team. Programmers write the computer code that makes the game world function. Artists draw and animate the characters and environments. Designers build fun and challenging levels and write the storyline. In addition, a production team manages the **schedule**, a QA (Quality Assurance) team tests the game, an audio team composes music and sound effects, and a marketing team gets the word out about the game to people like you. Paying all these employees is the highest cost.

THE LABOR MARKET

A game company wants highly skilled workers, and workers want high-paying jobs. Workers, or **labor**, "sell" their skills to companies in the **labor market**. Demand in this market refers to the number of jobs available for a certain type of worker. Supply is the number of workers with the right skills for that job.

Video game programming is a highly skilled job. Few people have the right skills, so supply is low. However, game companies need to hire a lot of programmers, so demand is high. This means that companies compete with one another to offer the best salaries to programmers. The opposite situation occurs with QA jobs. QA testers play the game to look for bugs, or problems with the game. A lot of people want to work in the games industry, but these positions don't require the special skills that programming jobs do. Companies don't have to pay as much to fill these positions because a lot of people compete for these jobs.

COST-BENEFIT DECISIONS

During production of a video game, the main goal is to build a fun game that many people will want to buy. But the company has a limited amount of time, money, and people. Not every fun idea makes it into the finished game. Let's say the ninja gecko team wanted to add jetpacks to the game but, after four months of work, the team still hasn't finished. Should it give up on the jetpacks?

The team has to make a **cost-benefit decision**. This type of decision looks at whether the costs of a choice are greater or less than the benefits. The money the company has already spent to pay employees to work on the jetpacks is a **sunk cost**—it can't get that money back. The time it will take to finish the jetpacks is an opportunity cost—the developers won't be able to spend that time on other parts of the game. The benefit is how many more people might buy the game if the geckos can move at top speed.

WHAT DO YOU THINK?

People make cost-benefit decisions all the time. Think about a difficult choice you made. What were the advantages and the drawbacks? How did you decide what to do?

GAME ENGINES

Game developers often have to build the tools they need before they can work on the game itself. Imagine that you wanted to cook a meal, but first you had to build your own stove, knives, pots, and pans! A game engine is a software program that provides tools to help designers, artists, and programmers to build new levels and animate characters.

A game engine can save a year or more of development time, but it is very expensive. Game companies have to compare the cost of the engine to the amount they would spend building their own tools.

TRICKS OF THE TRADE

Unreal Development Kit is a free version of the powerful Unreal Engine from Epic Games. More than one million people, from students to small companies, use Unreal Developer Kit to build games easily and quickly.

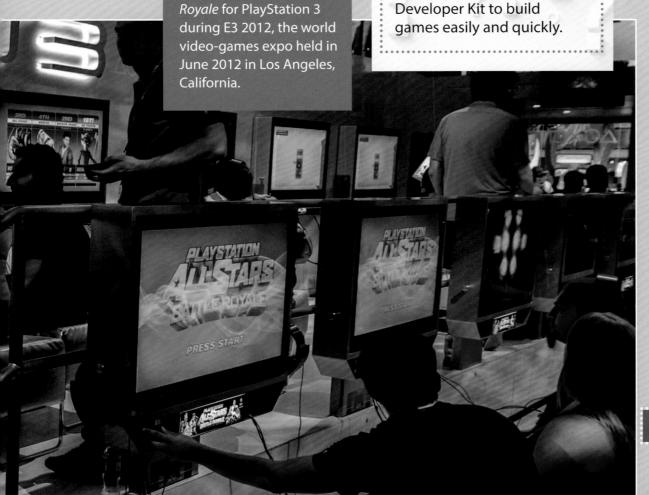

Players compete on *PlayStation All-Stars Battle Royale* for PlayStation 3 during E3 2012, the world video-games expo held in June 2012 in Los Angeles, California.

TIME ON THEIR HANDS

Console games take about two years to produce. The timeline begins with pre-production, when the core team plans the storyline, art style, and important features of the game. Development is the longest and most expensive part of the project. More people join the team at this stage to actually make the game. About halfway through, the focus shifts from adding new features to fixing features that already exist. The development team has to finish their work about four months before the release date so that there is plenty of time to have the game certified, manufactured, and shipped to stores.

INSIDER INSIGHT

"It's an art and a science trying to figure out exactly which features to keep, which to cut, and when to cut them."
Jen MacLean, game developer

Developers test a video game at the Ubisoft studio in France.

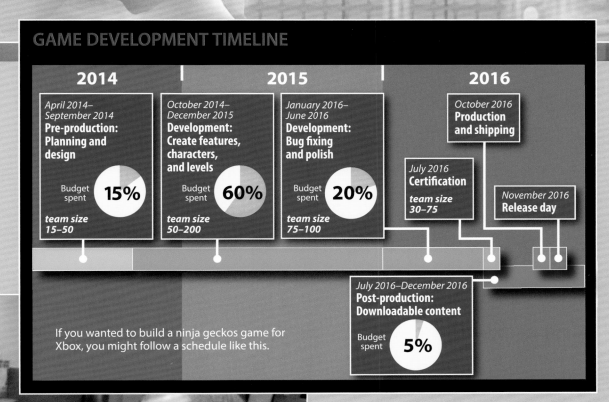

GAME DEVELOPMENT TIMELINE

2014

April 2014–September 2014
Pre-production: Planning and design

Budget spent **15%**

team size 15–50

2015

October 2014–December 2015
Development: Create features, characters, and levels

Budget spent **60%**

team size 50–200

January 2016–June 2016
Development: Bug fixing and polish

Budget spent **20%**

team size 75–100

2016

October 2016
Production and shipping

July 2016
Certification
team size 30–75

November 2016
Release day

July 2016–December 2016
Post-production: Downloadable content

Budget spent **5%**

If you wanted to build a ninja geckos game for Xbox, you might follow a schedule like this.

MORE PEOPLE, MORE PROBLEMS

When a lot of work needs to get done, it can help to hire more people, as long as the company has the budget and the space to do so. **Labor productivity** is the amount of work an average person gets done in one hour. If one game artist completes one character sketch every hour, then hiring three game artists could mean three sketches per hour.

But at some point, hiring more artists doesn't increase productivity. More people mean more meetings, more managers, and more communication problems. The task of getting a bunch of artists to work together can actually add more time to the project than those extra artists save. A smart company will hire more people only if doing so will increase the total work done.

4 RELEASE DAY

Release day is the moment when a new game becomes available for purchase. More than 100 people may put years of work and millions of dollars into a console video game. After all that, consumers like you decide the success of the project. Do you buy the game? Do you love it and tell all your friends?

ABOVE Distribution centers hold on to products until retail stores place an order.

The game *Just Dance 4* is revealed for the first time during E3 2012, the world video game expo in Los Angeles, California.

CERTIFICATION

Have you ever wondered why most Xbox games come in the same lime-green box? Before each Xbox game is released, it has to pass certification. Certification is a long test to make sure the game follows a set of rules that describe everything from design features of the packaging to the way the game menus work.

Console makers, including Microsoft, the company that makes the Xbox, run this test to ensure that all games for their system meet certain standards. If a game fails certification, the game company has to fix the problem, then the certification test begins all over again!

MANUFACTURING AND DISTRIBUTION

Once the game has passed certification, it is produced in mass quantities in factories and then packaged and shipped to stores. If all goes as planned, the games show up in stores on the release date. October through December is the busiest season for new video games. About half of the total game and console sales for the whole year happen during the holidays when people are buying gifts. Some companies choose not to release a game at this busy time simply because there is so much competition in the shops.

In the end, those shelves full of brand-new games represent a lot of resources. From the game company offices to the electricity that powered the programmers' computers and the plastic in the game packaging, each part of the process uses up money, time, and materials. Is it worth it? If enough people buy the game, yes!

BUILDING HYPE

Companies advertise new games and consoles at E3 2013 in Los Angeles, California.

GETTING TO KNOW YOU

Even an awesome game won't sell if nobody knows about it. The marketing team has an important job. They try to create "buzz" to get people talking about a new game weeks before release day. Marketing continues after the game comes out. A standard marketing budget is 15 percent of expected revenues. The larger the audience for the game, the higher the percentage spent on marketing. Some companies spend more on marketing than on development!

CREATING BUZZ

Television advertising is still one of the easiest ways to reach large numbers of consumers, but it isn't cheap. In 2013, an ad for the video game *Assassin's Creed 3* cost about $4 million to be aired during the Super Bowl. Spending that kind of money is rare. Almost all games are advertised online with trailers that reveal the story, style, and game-play. Game companies also attend trade shows or release demonstration models that let consumers play through part of the game for free.

Marketers provide previews of the game to journalists at gaming websites, magazines, and TV and radio stations. Once the game is out, online reviews share opinions about the game, and eye-catching displays at stores remind people to buy it.

A GOOD DEAL

Hundreds of companies are trying to create buzz for games at the same time. Monopolistic competition in the video game market means that most companies rely on advertising about game content, not price, to try to influence consumers' choices. Ads provide incentives or reasons to buy a product. Incredibly realistic or artistic art, a compelling story, or innovative game play can be incentives for dedicated gamers. Monetary incentives, such as a 25 percent discount or a special code to unlock extra content, make customers feel as though they're getting a good deal.

5 SELLING THE GAME

Stores carry hundreds of games. The app store on your phone or tablet offers thousands more. You can also download games on to your computer, Xbox, or PlayStation. Where do you go to shop for games? The markets for boxed games, free apps, and downloadable games are quite different. In each market, the money you spend on a game gets divided up among the companies who helped get the game into your hands.

PROMPTS TO BUY A GAME

Boxed games

44%	Heard about it from friends or family
41%	Saw a TV ad
38%	Saw it on a store shelf
11%	Played an online demo

Digital games

43%	Heard about it from friends or family
27%	Saw a TV ad
18%	Played an online demo

A prompt is something that gets you to do something, such as buy a video game.

Wii became popular for getting people off the couch and moving!

INCENTIVES

Advertisements can provide incentives, such as discounts, to help persuade you to buy a game. Many times, the factors that matter most in your decisions are more personal. If all of your friends are playing *Zuni and the Ninja Geckos*, you will probably want your own copy. The fun times you'll have playing the game with friends is a **positive incentive** to buy the game. But what if your parents won't let you buy a new game until you clean your room, and you really don't want to pick up your dirty socks? That's known as a **negative incentive**.

PRICE DISCRIMINATION

Okay, you've picked up your socks and emptied out your piggy bank. You have $54.37. Too bad! The ninja gecko game costs $59.99. Only people who are willing and able to spend that exact amount can have the game. Some people would pay more, while others can only afford a lower price.

Price discrimination happens when companies sell the same product or service for different prices in different situations. For example, movie theaters and theme parks often charge less for a kid's ticket than an adult's. It's often better for a company to make a sale at a lower price than to make no sale at all.

In the games industry, price discrimination can take place over time. Marketing campaigns get everyone psyched for release day. Fans have watched online game trailers and played through game teasers—they can't wait! On release day, a new console game usually costs $59.99. Over time, if the game doesn't sell very well, the game companies may lower the price.

BOXED GAMES

A MONOPOLY BUSINESS

Compared to other forms of entertainment, such as movies and books, brand new console video games are awfully expensive! Remember that game companies have a monopoly on each game they sell. If you want the new ninja gecko game, you can only buy it from one company. You have to pay the price that company sets, wait to see if the price drops, or wait for a used copy.

PRICE MAKERS

A company with a monopoly is a **price maker**—it can charge any amount for a game. In a more competitive market, different companies all offer the same product. To compete, they have to charge the lowest possible price that allows them to cover costs. These companies are known as **price takers**. Video-game companies argue that the reason for the steep price is the high cost of game development and the number of different companies that all share these costs. They also have to share the revenues, and they all want to make a profit.

ROYALTIES

Typically, the publisher collects revenues when retail stores buy games to put on their shelves. Then the publisher pays out royalties to the developer. A **royalty payment** is a set percentage of money that comes from the sale of intellectual property (I.P.). The creator of the work gets paid based on how many copies are sold. But in some deals, the creator has already received an advance against royalties, or an advance payment to help fund the project. This means that they won't earn any new money until sales reach the amount of the advance.

WHAT DO YOU THINK?

Do you think video game and console companies are price makers or price takers? Why?

THE RECORD BREAKERS

Intellectual property owners charge licensing fees to other companies that wish to create products, called merchandise, such as toys, backpacks, and clothing based on game worlds or characters. The company Rovio, maker of the mobile game *Angry Birds*, brought in $32 million from merchandising and licensing in 2011.

PROFITS FROM A CONSOLE GAME

Total $60

- Retail store $15
- Developer $12
- Manufacturing $3
- Publisher $20
- Console company $10

Who gets that $60 you spend on a new console game?

Consumers shop for the Wii U handheld game console in Tokyo, Japan.

FREE TO PLAY

DO FREE GAMES MAKE MONEY?

Open up the app store on any smartphone or tablet and type in "games." Chances are, quite a few of the games you find are free to download, or offer free and paid versions. Why in the world would a company give something away for free? Advertisements and **in-app purchases** both help free games make money. Other companies will pay to advertise their products on your screen for a few moments. But ads tend to interrupt the game and annoy players. In-app purchases that save time or allow players to customize the game are often more effective.

WELCOME IN THE WHALES

Many free games offer some form of currency, such as points, stars, or charms, that you can trade for items, hints, or custom features. You earn these points as you play the game. Or, you can get hundreds of points instantly if you pay for them with real money. Many people are patient enough that they never have to pay. But about two percent of people will spend a lot of money just to get through the game faster. The game industry calls these people "whales." If a free game can get a million downloads, then two percent of that number is 20,000 paying customers.

TRICKS OF THE TRADE

It's free to start playing the popular online multiplayer game *Star Wars: The Old Republic*. Players can change to a monthly subscription later or pay to unlock content as they go. "We wanted to allow players more freedom and choice in how they play (and pay for) our game," says Cory Butler of BioWare.

Before a new mobile device launches, the company often hires or invites developers to create games for the device. The games and the device are **complementary goods**, since each product makes the other more attractive to customers.

FREE-TO-PLAY MOBILE GAMES

$11.4 billion — expected revenues of the U.S. mobile gaming industry by 2014

51% of the top 25 top grossing games in the app store are free to play

50% of revenue from top grossing iPhone apps comes from in-app purchases

70–80% of all app downloads are games

81% of all app downloads are free

The free version of *Angry Birds* earns an estimated $1 million per month from in-game advertising

37% of iPhone owners play games every day

This list illustrates the rise of free-to-play mobile games.

The mobile phone game *Angry Birds* has been downloaded more than 600 million times.

WHAT DO YOU THINK?

How do deep discounts and limited-time sales help companies increase their profits in the long run?

In *AaaaaAAaaaAAAaaAAAAaAAAAA!!! for the Awesome* from Dejobaan games, players dodge obstacles as they fall through the sky.

MILLIONS OF DOWNLOADS

Each day people download about 24 million mobile games. Digital game stores, including Steam and Xbox live arcade, attract many paying customers. But sales of digital games represent just 40 percent of the market. Physical games still make more money.

In any store, position of a product matters a lot. You're more likely to buy a game that you see on the shelf at eye-level. In the digital market, the "shelves" may be as tiny as a cell-phone screen. Game developers compete for just a few top spots. In many digital stores, the number of downloads, average ratings, and prices determines the order.

GAINING STEAM

Steam, the most popular program for downloading and playing computer games, controls 51 percent of the market for digital games. Developers price their own games in a wide range from under $5 to more than $30. Steam takes 30 percent of each sale. Boxed game publishers may take 70 percent, so Steam offers a higher **profit margin** for developers who work independently.

Special promotions on the home screen or at the top of Steam search results can reach an audience of five million at peak hours. Valve, the company that runs Steam, regularly chooses games to feature with deep discounts. These promotions lead to a huge boost in sales. During a special 75-percent-off "flash deal," a company may sell 60 times the usual number of games. These limited-time sales create a sense of urgency that enhances the power of the economic incentive. Increased downloads mean more people know about the game and may tell their friends. This often helps to increase demand for the game.

Independent game developers need to get Valve's attention in order to receive a promotion spot and reach their audience. So they try to create buzz on gaming websites and in the game industry. They need to stand out from the crowd.

TRICKS OF THE TRADE

The entire cost of an independent game project generally equals about two hours of development time at a large game studio! Digital game stores allow tiny companies with small budgets to reach a larger audience than ever before.

PIRACY AND USED GAMES

THE USED GAMES MARKET

If you can't afford a new console game, just wait. In a week or two, somebody else will finish playing and sell the game back to the store. About 80 million used game discs are sold each year, compared to more than 400 million new games. Game publishers and developers dislike the used game market because they don't make any money on a used game sale. They are trying to change this situation by including special codes in new games.

Some game studios claim that used game sales hurt their business more than piracy.

WHAT DO YOU THINK?

Illegal online file-sharing sites offer pirated copies of games, music, and movies. It is a form of stealing to download any of these products. Do you agree?

These codes work only once to unlock certain content. If you buy the game used, you also have to buy a new code to access the full game.

A GAMING GOLDMINE

For retailers like GameStop, the used game market is a goldmine. When GameStop sells a new title, the profit margin is about 25 percent. But if the customer brings that same game back again and trades it in for store credits, GameStop can sell the disc again at almost 100 percent profit!

In the weeks after release day, used sales hurt game companies the most. During this time the games are only marked down a small amount and most buyers likely would have bought the game new. But in general, people who buy used games are bargain hunters or consumers who can't afford new games. And people who trade in used games tend to spend the money on more new games. GameStop reports that 70 percent of game trade-in money goes toward new game purchases.

Used games can also increase brand loyalty among a larger audience. Cheap used games attract new customers, who might buy new future sequels or game merchandise.

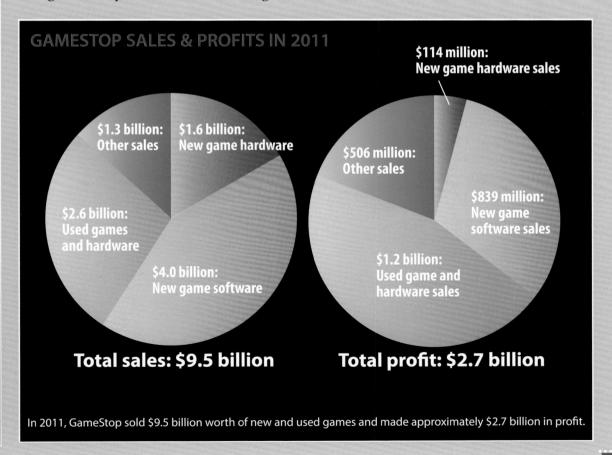

GAMESTOP SALES & PROFITS IN 2011

$1.3 billion: Other sales

$1.6 billion: New game hardware

$2.6 billion: Used games and hardware

$4.0 billion: New game software

Total sales: $9.5 billion

$114 million: New game hardware sales

$506 million: Other sales

$839 million: New game software sales

$1.2 billion: Used game and hardware sales

Total profit: $2.7 billion

In 2011, GameStop sold $9.5 billion worth of new and used games and made approximately $2.7 billion in profit.

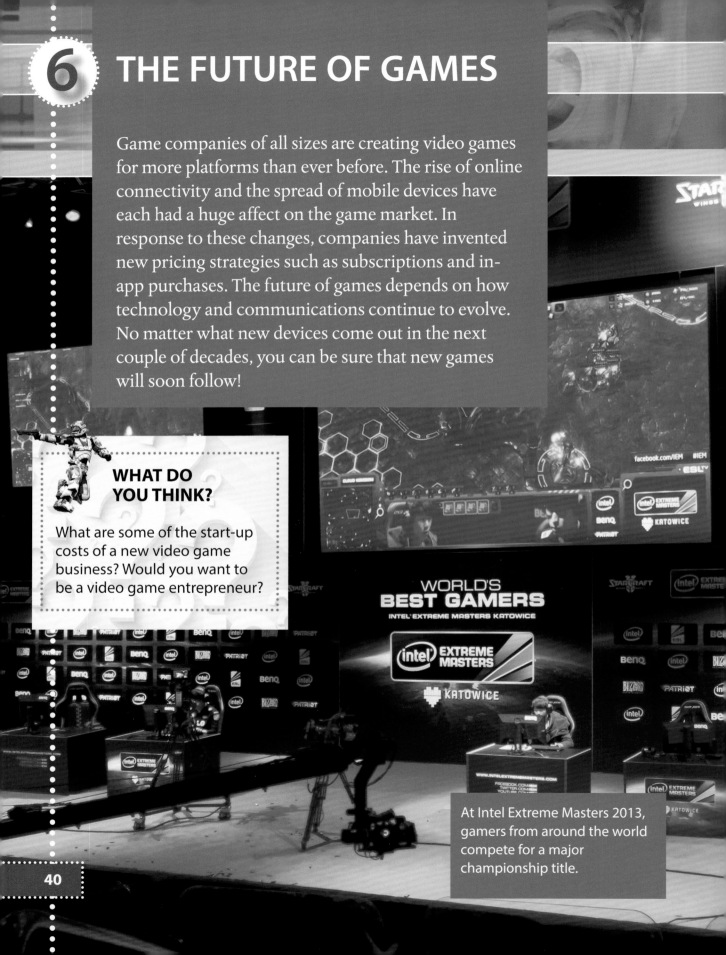

6 THE FUTURE OF GAMES

Game companies of all sizes are creating video games for more platforms than ever before. The rise of online connectivity and the spread of mobile devices have each had a huge affect on the game market. In response to these changes, companies have invented new pricing strategies such as subscriptions and in-app purchases. The future of games depends on how technology and communications continue to evolve. No matter what new devices come out in the next couple of decades, you can be sure that new games will soon follow!

WHAT DO YOU THINK?

What are some of the start-up costs of a new video game business? Would you want to be a video game entrepreneur?

At Intel Extreme Masters 2013, gamers from around the world compete for a major championship title.

DO YOU HAVE A GREAT GAME IDEA?

You could turn your idea into a business some day. The economy depends on creative risk-takers to develop new products and services. **Entrepreneurs** are people who pull resources like land, labor, and capital together to create a business. But being an entrepreneur isn't easy!

Start-up costs are a big barrier to entry for any new business. Before a new game company can start operating, the founders have to pay for computers and software programs, and hire designers, programmers, and artists. Entrepreneurs take on these costs themselves (or seek outside funding) because they believe that they will make more money in the long run than it will cost to stay in business.

START-UP COSTS

The start-up costs for game development are cheaper now than ever before. People can download free software and build games at home. However, it still takes a lot of hard work to make a stand-out game. The time a developer puts into a new game business is time he or she can't spend earning a paycheck at a regular job. The money a developer could earn elsewhere is the opportunity cost of an independent project.

An increasing number of students are studying game development. Many will look for jobs in the game industry when they graduate and some will start their own businesses. The hard truth is that about half of new businesses fail. What does it take to succeed? Some of the secrets of successful entrepreneurs are: hard work, innovation, organization, sound economic decision-making, and a lot of luck.

THE RECORD BREAKERS

The company Valve created *Portal*, an innovative and award-winning game. Players solve puzzles using a portal gun that can open doors between the floor, ceiling, and walls. Valve also owns the Steam store and makes more profit per employee than the search engine giant Google. Valve can afford to take a risk with a totally new game experience. With *Portal*, the risk was well worth it!

A CONSTANT CONNECTION

New game consoles and other devices will be connected to the Internet all of the time. Game companies are already taking advantage of this constant connection with and between players.

After a game comes out, new downloadable content and expansion packs help keep enthusiasm high for a game. This extra content costs the company far less to develop than the original game world, so they can sell it at a higher profit. Players enjoy these content releases because they get to explore new levels or try new characters.

A GAME ECONOMY

New technology may change the way games look and feel. Increased connectivity may change the way you pay for games and how much you pay, but the basic rules of economics will remain the same.

Many games contain scarce resources such as magical items, gold, or gems. Players can shop for items and prices follow the laws of supply and demand. Some games allow players to set up businesses, grow crops, or hire armies. Incentives, sunk costs, and opportunity costs influence the choices players make during the game.

If you understand economics and how the economy works, you'll make better, more informed decisions—both inside and outside the game world.

TRICKS OF THE TRADE

Games are getting easier and easier to make. All you need to get started is a program like GameMaker or Sploder. If you want to work in the game industry some day, start making games now to improve your skills and your eventual chance for success.

You can make your own fantasy world on a computer program.

A parent and child use a tablet together. Future device screens could take up an entire wall—or fold up inside your pocket.

WHAT DO YOU THINK?

How is a game economy like the real economy? Think about a game you love to play. Can you buy and sell things in the game? What makes some items more valuable than others?

GLOSSARY

brand The name of a product, design, or character produced by a company

capital A human-made resource that is used to produce other things

capitalism A system of economics in which individuals, not governments, control most businesses and resources

competition The economic battle between companies trying to sell the same types of products

complementary goods Two products purchased or used together

consumers People who purchase goods and services

consumer sovereignty The idea that people's choices of what to buy determine what companies produce

cost Money spent

cost-benefit decision A choice made after comparing possible positive and negative outcomes

demand The amount of a service or good that people buy at a certain price

economics Study of the economy

elasticity A measure of how much supply or demand changes when price changes

entrepreneur Person who takes the risk to start a new business

funding Money supplied to help a new business or project get started

goods Physical products that are bought and sold in an economy

human capital The people who work on a product

in-app purchases Points or features bought with real money while playing a mobile game application

incentive A possible outcome that influences a purchase decision

intellectual property Ideas that belong to a certain person or company

labor Workers that produce goods and services

labor market Where workers seek jobs and companies seek workers

labor productivity Amount of work an average person does in one hour

law of diminishing returns If a project isn't changing in size, each person added to the project completes less work.

licensing fee Money paid to an owner of intellectual property for the right to use that property in products

GLOSSARY

market economy A system in which people and businesses make decisions freely about what to buy and sell

monopolistic competition Rivalry between companies that sell products that are similar, but not identical

monopoly A market controlled by just one company

oligopoly A market controlled by a small group of companies

opportunity cost The value of the option that wasn't chosen in a decision

physical capital Tools or machines used to create products

positive or negative incentive A possible good or bad outcome that influences a consumer to buy or not to buy something

price discrimination The practice of charging different prices for the same product or service

price maker A company that is able to set any price it desires and still compete

price takers Companies that must set prices based on the market to compete

producers Manufacturers or financiers of products

profit Money gained when revenues are higher than costs

profit margin The percentage of revenues that is left after subtracting costs

resources The basic components of all goods and services

revenue Total money received from the sales of goods or services

revenue share Income received as a percentage or share of the total money a company makes

royalty payment A set percentage of money from the sale of a product that goes to an intellectual property owner

scarcity The lack of resources to meet everyone's needs or desires

schedule A timetable of action

services Activities or experiences that are bought and sold in an economy

sunk cost Money that has already been paid

supply The amount of a good or service that companies produce at a certain price

FIND OUT MORE

BOOKS TO READ

Acton, Johnny, and David Goldblatt. *Eyewitness Books: Economy.* Dorling Kindersley, 2010.

Andrews, Carolyn. *What Are Goods and Services?* (Economics in Action). Crabtree Publishing, 2008.

Challen, Paul. *What Is Supply and Demand?* (Economics in Action). Crabtree Publishing, 2010.

Flatt, Lizann. *The Economics of the Super Bowl* (Economics of Entertainment). Crabtree Publishing, 2013.

Girard Golomb, Kristen. *Economics and You, Grades 5–8.* Mark Twain Media, 2012.

Hollander, Barbara. *Money Matters: An Introduction to Economics.* Heinemann Raintree, 2010.

Johnson, Robin. *The Economics of Making a Movie* (Economics of Entertainment). Crabtree Publishing, 2013.

Perl, Sheri. *The Economics of a Rock Concert* (Economics of Entertainment). Crabtree Publishing, 2013.

WEBSITES

http://dailyinfographic.com/
Information of all types presented visually

www.scholastic.com/browse/collection.jsp?id=455
Articles and activities about the economy

www.socialstudiesforkids.com/subjects/economics.htm
An overview of economics

www.gamasutra.com
The art and business of making games

MOVIE

Sundance award-winning documentary about independent game development
Indie Game: The Movie directed by Lisanne Pajot and James Swirsky

INDEX

REFERENCES

ACKNOWLEDGMENTS

The author wishes to thank the following people for assistance, and credit these sources of information:

Personal Interviews:
Liam Callahan, Games industry analyst; Ichiro Lambe, Independent game developer; Michael Pachter, Games industry analyst; David Riley, Games industry analyst; Representatives from BioWare, Epic Games, Valve.

Book:
Kruger, Alan B. and David A. Anderson, *Explorations in Economics*, BFW/Worth Publishers: New York, NY, 2013.

Websites:
www.dailyinfographic.com
www.penny-arcade.com
www.computerandvideogames.com
www.digitaltrends.com
www.escapistmagazine.com
www.esrb.org   www.eurogamer.net
www.ft.com   www.gamasutra.com
www.gamingupdate.com
 www.gartner.com
www.ign.com   www.joystiq.com
www.kotaku.com   www.nintendo.com
www.npd.com   www.pcgamer.com:
www.vgchartz.com

Industry Reports and Article:
O'Donnell, Casey. "The North American Game Industry," 2011.
Pham, Alex, and Ben Fritz. "Activision Bungie contract unsealed in Call of Duty case," *Los Angeles Times*, May 21, 2012.
Plumer, Brad. "The Economics of Video Games," *The Washington Post*, September 28, 2012.
Zackariasson, Peter. "Basics in the Marketing of Video Games," 2009.
Essential Facts About the Computer and Video Game Industry: 2013 Sales, Demographic and Usage Data, Entertainment Software Association, 2013.
"Game Developer Salary Survey," Game Developer Magazine, April 2013.
"Games Market Dynamics," The NPD Group/Retail Tracking Service, 2012.
US Gaming: A 360° View, The Nielsen Company, 2012.

Movie:
Indie Game: The Movie, 2012.